HEALING YOUR
GRIEVING HEART
FOR TEENS

Also by Alan Wolfelt:

Creating Meaningful Funeral Ceremonies:
A Guide for Families

Healing a Child's Grieving Heart:
100 Practical Ideas for Families, Friends
and Caregivers

Healing a Friend's Grieving Heart:
100 Practical Ideas for Helping Someone
You Love Through Loss

Healing a Teen's Grieving Heart:
100 Practical Ideas for Families, Friends
and Caregivers

Healing Your Grieving Heart for Kids:
100 Practical Ideas

The Journey Through Grief:
Reflections on Healing

Understanding Your Grief: Ten Essential
Touchstones For Finding Hope
and Healing Your Heart

*Companion Press is dedicated to the education and
support of both the bereaved and bereavement caregivers.*

*We believe that those who companion the bereaved by
walking with them as they journey in grief have a
wondrous opportunity: to help others embrace and grow
through grief—and to lead fuller, more deeply-lived lives
themselves because of this important ministry.*

Companion
P R E S S

For a complete catalog and
ordering information, write or call:

Companion Press
The Center for Loss and Life Transition
3735 Broken Bow Road
Fort Collins, CO 80526
(970) 226-6050
www.centerforloss.com

HEALING YOUR GRIEVING HEART
For Teens

•

100 PRACTICAL IDEAS

•

ALAN D. WOLFELT, PH.D.

Companion
PRESS

Fort Collins, Colorado
An imprint of the Center for Loss and Life Transition

Companion Press is an imprint of the
Center for Loss and Life Transition,
3735 Broken Bow Road, Fort Collins, Colorado 80526

Companion Press books may be purchased in bulk for sales promotions, premiums or fundraisers. Please contact the publisher at the above address for more information.

Printed in the United States of America

16 15   8

ISBN 978-1-879651-23-4

To my precious daughter Megan. Thanks for inspiring me to write this book that will help teens mourn well so they can live well and love well.

"I've seen fire and I've seen rain.
I've seen sunny days that I thought would never end.
I've seen lonely times when I could not find a friend.
But I always thought that I would see you again."

James Taylor

Introduction

Because you are a teen and because you're unique, you're very special. This is an exciting stage of your life. The changes you're going through physically, emotionally, intellectually, and spiritually can be exhilarating and also overwhelming. You're not a kid anymore. You're not an adult either. Others may expect you to act, think, and feel like an adult, but much of your childhood, thankfully, is still alive inside you.

So when someone you love dies, it can be more difficult for you now than at any other age. It's hard to understand and cope with all the feelings that accompany grief along with the changes your body and mind are experiencing. In some ways these feelings are similar: Both can cause your moods to swing unexpectedly. Both can make you feel out of control of your life.

I'm sorry you've lost someone who meant a lot to you. You may feel very sad or hurt right now. Perhaps you're angry. Or depressed. Maybe you feel lost or deserted. All these feelings are part of grieving and are OK to feel.

Let me explain the difference between grief and mourning. Grief is what you think and feel on the inside when someone you love dies. Mourning is the expression of those thoughts and feelings—letting them out somehow. You mourn when you talk to other people about your grief, write about it in a journal, cry, look at photos of the person who died, visit the cemetery, etc. You may be grieving like crazy inside but unless you let out those powerful, painful thoughts and feelings—unless you mourn—you won't truly heal.

Sean Covey wrote a book called *The 7 Habits of Highly Effective Teens* (a good book, by the way). In it, he talks about the concept of a Personal Bank Account, or PBA. Your PBA is not for money, it's where you store your emotional well-being and self-esteem. Every time you do something good for your emotional health (like helping someone else or being honest), you make a deposit. Every time you compromise your emotional health (say by cheating or being mean to someone), you make a withdrawal. The idea is the higher the balance in your PBA, the happier you'll be.

Since you're in grief now, I'd like you to think of yourself as having a Personal Mourning Account, or a PMA. Every time you express your thoughts and feelings related to your grief, you make a deposit. Every time you repress your thoughts and feelings (or express them in unhealthy ways, like doing drugs or hurting yourself), you make a huge withdrawal. Your goal is to grow your PMA balance, slowly and over time and with the support and love of those around you. It's OK to make withdrawals once in a while; we all repress our feelings or do stupid things sometimes. But if you make more deposits than withdrawals, you'll grow to reconcile your loss and find meaning in life and living again.

Another important way to make PMA deposits is to let others help you with your grief. Now I understand that you may not want help. When you're a teenager, one of your main tasks in life is to become more independent and handle things on your own. Nature designed it that way so that you'll learn to fend for and make a life for yourself. But grief is an exception; you can't cope with it alone (nobody can, not even adults) and you shouldn't try to. You need to let others be there for you right now. Open up to your parents or other caring adults when they want to talk about the death. If you don't want to talk about it, at least spend time with them. Talk to your friends. Talk to your coach. Talk to your teacher. Join a support group for grieving teens. Even when others don't know what to say or say the wrong things, know that they care about you and want to help.

The 100 ideas in this book are designed to help you grow your PMA. Each page also has a section called "Express Yourself," which offers a practical suggestion for something you can do right now to help deal with your feelings. When you acknowledge, experience and express the feelings that accompany grief, you grow your PMA and you begin to heal.

You'll notice that many of the "Express Yourself" ideas suggest writing in a journal. This is an excellent way for many teens to do the work of mourning. Journaling is private and independent, yet it's still expressing your grief outside of yourself. If you don't think of yourself as a journaler, I encourage you to give it a try anyway. You might find it works really well for you right now. Alternatives to journaling include creating artwork, spending time in nature, playing or listening to music and, of course, sharing your thoughts and feelings with people who care about you.

Keep this book close by. Refer to it often as you go through the painful and healing process of grief. Refer to it again when you want to be there for someone else who is grieving.

Please take good care of yourself and be patient. Time, too, is a great healer. With time and the support of others as well as growth of your PMA, you'll again feel hope and a renewed zest for life. And it may be hard to believe this now, but you'll also emerge wiser, more sensitive, and more complete than you were before. Believe in yourself. Believe in your ability to grow and heal. Believe in God's plan for you on this earth. Good luck and godspeed.

All the best,

1.
Understand the difference between grief and mourning.

- Grief is what you think and feel on the inside when someone you love dies. It's numbness, sadness, anger, guilt, and sometimes relief, all rolled up into one. It's a pain in your gut and a hole in your chest.

- Mourning is expressing your grief, letting it out somehow. You mourn when you cry, talk about the death, write about it, punch a pillow.

- Everybody grieves inside when someone they love dies. But only people who mourn really heal and move on to live and love fully again.

- This book does two things: It teaches you about grief and gives you mourning ideas. Mourning is awesome. Really. It's powerful and it's the only thing that works.

Express yourself:
What feelings are you having right now about the death? Express them right this minute by writing them down or by telling someone. How do you feel now that you've done a bit of mourning?

2.
Understand the concept of "reconciliation."

- Sometimes you'll hear people talk about "recovering" from grief. I don't like this term because it implies that grief is an illness that must be cured. Grief is not an illness but a natural and necessary process.

- Besides, you don't "recover" from or "get over" grief. Instead, you become "reconciled" to it. In other words, you learn to live with it and are forever changed by it.

- This does not mean a life of misery, however. We often not only heal but grow through grief. Our lives can potentially be deeper and more meaningful after the death of someone loved.

- Reconciliation takes time. You may not become truly reconciled to your loss for several years and even then you may have "griefbursts" forever.

Express yourself:
Talk to someone who's experienced the death of someone she loved. Ask her how she survived and if she's "recovered" from the deaths. Her story may help you understand that though grief is forever, it softens over time and that life can be joyful once more.

3.

Attend the funeral or memorial service.

- Rituals allow us to honor and memorialize someone who's died. It may seem difficult to face going to a funeral or memorial service. But participating in such an event will help you acknowledge the loss and begin to reconcile yourself to it.

- There's comfort in knowing that others share your loss, and the support of others can help you through your grief.

- Being part of a memorial ritual helps dose you with the reality of the death and melt feelings of denial or disbelief you may have experienced when you first learned of the death.

- You can participate in the funeral by doing a reading, playing music, creating a personalized program on your computer, lighting a candle or placing something special inside the casket.

Express yourself:
Say goodbye to the person who died. Let him know that you will miss him and keep memories of him alive.

4.
UNDERSTAND THE SIX
NEEDS OF MOURNING

Need 1. Accept the reality of the death.

- Someone you love has died and can never come back. That's a really hard thing to accept, but it's true.

- It may take you weeks, even months, to really accept the fact that this person is gone. It's normal for it to take that long.

- First you'll come to accept the death intellectually, with your head. Only over time will you come to fully accept it with your heart.

- Now and then, especially at first, you may push away or deny the reality to yourself. That's also normal. You'll accept the reality, bit by bit, as you're ready.

Express yourself:
Tell someone about the death today. Talking about it will help you
work on this important first step to reconciling your loss.

5.

UNDERSTAND THE SIX NEEDS OF MOURNING

Need 2. Let yourself feel the pain of the loss.

• You need to let yourself feel the pain of your loss. You need to feel it before you can heal it.

• Of course, it's easier to avoid, repress, deny or push away the pain of grief than it is to confront it. The problem is, confronting it is what tames it. If you don't confront it, it will lurk forever in your heart and soul.

• You will probably need to "dose" yourself with your painful thoughts and feelings. In other words, you'll need to let just a little in at a time. If you were to try to allow in all the pain at once, you couldn't survive.

Express yourself:

Writing about your pain is a good way to let yourself feel it. Try keeping a journal during the next few months. Write in it every day after school or before bed. If you don't want to write a lot, that's OK. A few sentences a day is fine.

6.
UNDERSTAND THE SIX NEEDS OF MOURNING

Need 3. Remember the person who died.

- When someone you love dies, that person lives on in you through memory.

- To reconcile your loss, you need to actively remember the person who died and commemorate the life that was lived. Talk about the person who died. Use his name. Look at pictures of him.

- Never let anyone try to take away your memories in a misguided attempt to save you from pain. You need to remember, not to forget.

- Remembering the past makes hoping for the future possible.

Express yourself:
Brainstorm a list of characteristics or memories of the person who died. Write as fast as you can for 10 minutes (or more), then put away your list and look at it again another day.

7.
UNDERSTAND THE SIX
NEEDS OF MOURNING

Need 4. Develop a new self-identity.

- The person who died was part of who you are. Part of your identity came from this person.

- Let's say your best friend was Chris and she died. You probably thought of yourself not only as a son or daughter, a sibling, and a student but also as "Chris' best friend." Others thought of you in this way, too.

- The way you defined yourself and the way society defines you has changed.

- Now you need to re-adjust your self-identity, to re-anchor yourself. This is really hard, especially if the person who died played a big part in your life.

Express yourself:
What role did the person who died play in your life? How has your life changed because of the death? Write the answers to these questions in your journal.

8.
UNDERSTAND THE SIX
NEEDS OF MOURNING

Need 5. Search for meaning.

- When someone we love dies, we naturally question the meaning and purpose of life and death. Why do people die? Why did this person have to die? What happens to people after they die? Why am I still alive? What's life for?

- This may be the first time in your life that you've really thought about these questions. And questions just don't get any harder than these.

- Nobody really knows all the answers to these kinds of questions, not even grown-ups. But it's OK to ask adults you care about and trust what they think.

- Some adults have lived enough, loved enough, experienced enough and pondered enough to have some pretty good ideas. Hearing their philosophies might help you right now. Telling them what you think might help, too.

Express yourself:
Ask a parent or another adult you trust the "meaning of life and death" questions that are most on your mind right now. Listen to what they have to say without thinking you need to agree. You don't.

9.
UNDERSTAND THE SIX
NEEDS OF MOURNING

Need 6. Let others help you, now and always.

• When you're a teenager, it's natural to want adults to keep out of your face. You're getting old enough now that you don't need or want their help with every little thing, right?

• I agree with you. Growing up means finding your own way and doing things on your own.

• BUT, grief isn't an "on your own" kind of deal. It's probably the hardest work anyone ever has to do. And you just can't do it all on your own.

• Talk to adults who care about you. If you don't want to talk to them, at least let them talk to you. Or hang out with them without talking. Talk to your friends, instead. Join a support group. E-mail your thoughts and feelings to someone you don't have to look at every day.

Express yourself:
Who is the one person you could talk to about this death
and your grief if you really tried? Even if talking about your
feelings doesn't come easy to you, I beg you to give it a try,
one time, to this one person.

10.
Tell the story, over and over again if you need to.

- Acknowledging a death is a painful, ongoing need that we accomplish in doses, over time. For many mourners, "telling the story" of the death helps them learn to accept it.

- How and why did this person die? You might feel the need to talk this over with your friends or a trusted adult many, many times. This is normal.

- Or maybe you keep rerunning the story of the death in your mind instead of out loud. Thinking about it is also normal but talking about it will help you reconcile yourself to it.

Express yourself:
Tell the story of the death today to someone who cares about you.
Express any lingering questions or fears. If you just can't bring yourself to talk about it, write about it instead.

11.
Use the name of the person who died.

- When you're talking about the death or about your life in general, don't avoid using the name of the person who died. It's good to say the name out loud. It may feel weird at first but you'll get used to it.

- Using the name lets others know they can use it, too.

- Your friends and family may avoid saying the name of the person who died because they're afraid it will cause you pain. Let them know you like it when they talk about the person who died.

Express yourself:
Write the name of the person who died vertically in your journal, one letter per line. Then write a paragraph or poem about the person using these letters as the first letter in each line. Don't worry about finding the perfect words; just let your thoughts flow.

12.
Keep a journal.

- A journal is a wonderful way to record the events in your life and to deal with overwhelming or conflicting feelings. Writing about them in a journal no one else will see lets you sort through and express your feelings.

- Remember—your inner thoughts and feelings of grief need to be expressed outwardly (which includes writing) for you to reconcile your loss.

- Spend a few minutes each morning writing in your journal to clear your mind for the day. Write in it again before you go to bed.

Express yourself:

Find a journal and a new pen that are pleasing to you in size, shape, feel, and color. Start by writing the date and then the first thoughts that come to mind. Keep your hand moving. The words and thoughts will come.

13.

Keep a memento of the person who died.

- While the person who died is no longer with you physically, you can still keep a part of her with you as a reminder of the special relationship you had. A key, a piece of jewelry, an article of clothing or a lock of hair inside a locket, a trinket, or a special letter or card are all small enough to fit in your pocket or purse, so you can always carry a memory of that person with you. I wear my dad's watch everywhere I go.

- I sometimes call these items "linking objects" because they continue to link you to the person who died. If anyone tells you that finding comfort in such objects is morbid or "weak," don't listen. It's actually healthy and helpful. My dad's watch brings me great comfort. I hope you have something that gives you comfort, too.

Express yourself:

Choose a small object that is a comforting reminder of the person who died. Attach it to a set of keys or a necklace chain, or place it in a special container that you can keep with you all the time.

14.
Keep promises to yourself.

- Trust yourself in your grief journey. You are the only one who knows what it feels like for you.

- So, it's up to you to think of ways to help yourself. This book gives you a bunch of ideas, but you'll learn how to cope with your grief in ways that work for you.

- Be honest with yourself. If you need help, get it.

- Make some grief groundrules for yourself. Promise yourself you'll talk to your parents about your grief, for example, and then keep that promise.

Express yourself:
Promise yourself you'll mourn (not just grieve) this death whenever thoughts and feelings arise. Keep your promise.

15.
Let yourself feel numb.

- If the death was recent, you're probably feeling shocked and numb. You may feel nothing at all for a while.

- Most people feel this way after a death. It's nature's way (and maybe God's way) of protecting us, at first, from the full reality of the death.

- You might think, "I will wake up and this will not have happened." Early grief can feel like a dream.

- Your emotions need time to catch up with what your mind has been told. Let them come little by little.

Express yourself:
If you're feeling shock, numbness or disbelief, tell someone you trust. Expressing these feelings will help you see how normal and necessary they are.

16.
Live life in slow-mo.

- Sometimes it seems as though the world stops when someone we love dies. Part of that comes from our shock and disbelief. Part of it is the finality of death: This person is physically gone forever.

- In the days right after a person dies, you may find that life slows down. Moments may become extended, sounds muffled or amplified, sights blurred or crystallized. The world and your relation to it assumes a dreamlike, or spiritual, quality.

- Shock and numbness are nature's way of protecting us from terrible realities. Little by little your life will speed up again as you are able to dose yourself with the full reality of the death.

Express yourself:
Let yourself live in slow motion. Be attuned to the moments and sensations you feel. Share these experiences with a friend or family member.

17.

Let go of destructive myths about grief and mourning.

- Without knowing it, you may have bought into some of society's harmful myths about grief and mourning:
  - You need to be strong and carry on.
  - Tears are a sign of weakness.
  - You need to get over your grief.
  - You're the man/woman of the house now (if a parent has died).
  - Death is something we don't talk about.

- Not only are these statements not true, they're harmful.

- Sometimes these myths may make you feel guilty about or ashamed of your true thoughts and feelings.

- Your grief is your grief. It's normal and necessary. Allow it to be what it is.

Express yourself:

Do you think "being strong" after a death is a good thing? Flip that thinking around by remembering this: You're strong if you mourn because mourning is hard work, emotionally, physically and spiritually.

18.
Move toward your grief, not away from it.

- Our society isn't very good at confronting painful emotions. We think that it's better to run away from them than turn and face them.

- But in order to heal, you actually do need to move toward your grief instead of running away from it.

- As Helen Keller once said, "The only way to get to the other side is to go through the door."

- Let yourself feel your grief. When painful thoughts and feelings emerge, don't distract yourself with busyness and activities. Instead, focus on your pain.

Express yourself:
Today, make a conscious effort to think about the death and how it makes you feel. Allow yourself at least 10 full minutes to feel it before moving on with your busy day.

19.
Expect all kinds of feelings.

- You'll probably feel lots of different feelings in the coming weeks and months. You'll feel sad, of course, but you may also feel numb, angry, guilty, afraid, confused and even relieved and happy. All these feelings are normal. Experiencing them means you are mourning very well.

- Sometimes these feelings follow each other within a short period of time or they may occur simultaneously.

- Allow yourself to feel whatever it is you are feeling without judging yourself. There is no right or wrong way to feel after a death.

Express yourself:
In your journal or on a scrap of paper, write down all the feelings you've had since the death. Make two columns:
1) How I've Felt and 2) Why I Think I've Felt This Way.
Write down whatever comes into your head and heart. Now, find someone you trust to explore and sort through them.

20.

Don't expect yourself to mourn in a certain way or in a certain time.

- Your unique grief journey will be shaped by many factors, including:
    - the kind of relationship you had with the person who died.
    - the age of the person who died.
    - the circumstances of the death.
    - your unique personality.
    - your cultural background.
    - your religious or spiritual beliefs.
    - your gender.
    - your support systems.

- Because of these and other factors, no two deaths are ever mourned in precisely the same way.

- Don't think you should grieve in a certain way. Your grief is what it is. It's your right to express it.

Express yourself:

Draw two columns on a page in your journal. Title the left column "What I thought grief would be like." Title the right column "What it's really like." Fill both columns with your thoughts and feelings.

21.
Know that your relationship was unique.

- You're probably not the only one mourning this death. Others share your sorrow, and there's comfort in knowing they do.

- But it's also comforting to know that the relationship you had with the person who died was unique. You behaved differently around one another than you did around other people. You affected each other in different ways.

- You're a different human being now than if you had never known that person. Your life is enriched forever.

Express yourself:
Talk to a friend about the ways the person who died affected you. Identify the ways you've grown or become who you are as a result of having known that person.

22.
Cry.

- Crying is one of the best ways to express your grief—in other words, to mourn. Letting yourself cry is healthy. It's good therapy, too.

- You may have heard others talk about "being strong," and holding in tears when you're sad. But, in fact, your grief journey will be easier if you allow yourself to cry.

- Who do you feel comfortable crying in the presence of? A parent? A friend? A coach? Next time you need to cry, try to be near this person. She'll be a comforting presence.

- If you don't feel like crying, that's OK, too. Not everyone is a crier.

Express yourself:

If you feel the need to cry while you're at school or work, excuse yourself and go to a place where you can cry. Then wipe your tears, drink some water and return to what you were doing. If others ask what's wrong, it's sufficient to say that you were feeling sad and needed some quiet time.

23.
Laugh with friends.

- Laughter is one of life's greatest joys and best therapies. It's even better if it's shared. Make plans to get together with your friends for a day or evening of silliness. The more ideas you come up with, the more occasions you can plan to bring on the laughter.

- Play a harmless prank on someone. Commit to memory a few good jokes.

- Who makes you laugh? Spend time with that person.

Express yourself:

Dress up in funky clothes, rent or go to a funny movie or play, have a slumber party, share stories about funny or embarrassing moments in your life. Do whatever it takes to laugh until your stomach hurts.

24.
Don't let other kids
get to you.

- Some of your friends won't know how to talk to you about the death. They may say unkind things or they may ignore you.

- Knowing what to do or say when a friend is grieving is hard. It's hard for adults and even harder for young people. Give your friends a break if they're acting weird around you.

- Maybe you have one particular friend who's in-tune with your feelings and seems OK talking to you about the death or being with you even when you feel sad. Spend some extra time with this friend in the coming weeks and months.

Express yourself:
Identify one friend about your age you can talk to about this death.
See if talking to her helps you feel better.

25.
Take it easy on yourself.

- This book is supposed to help you deal with your grief and feel better, right? Well, that's not easy.

- Your grief journey will be hard. And your grief will probably feel worse before it feels better.

- Being a teenager is tough. It's a difficult time of life the way it is. Having to cope with the death of someone you love AND the normal parts of growing up at the same time can feel overwhelming.

- Take it easy on yourself, especially for the next few months. Don't set your expectations too high. Allow yourself to feel what you feel and think what you think. Give yourself a break when you're feeling low or too stressed.

Express yourself:
What's your daily schedule like? If it's jam-packed, now might be a good time to lighten your load. Talk to your teachers about deferring some schoolwork or cut back on your hours if you have a part-time job.

26.
Go with the flow.

- Allowing yourself some down-time right after the death is an important part of grieving. I often say to mourners: Your job right now is to just breathe in and breathe out. Eventually, though, you'll need to get back to your daily activities.

- Allowing yourself to get on with your life a little at a time is a big step towards reconciling your loss. Instead of avoiding your obligations, encourage yourself to do what you're supposed to be doing, one activity at a time—and then go with the flow.

Express yourself:
At the end of the day, write about when you were absorbed in a particular activity. Were you able to "lose yourself" by being immersed in something you enjoyed or that required your concentration?

27.
Drink lots of water.

- When you're grieving, you sometimes don't think about drinking enough. You simply may not feel thirsty.

- But your body still needs water. Dehydration can make you feel more tired and confused. Your brain doesn't function as well when it's dehydrated.

- Drink at least 4-5 glasses of water each day. Soda doesn't count. (In fact, soda depletes your calcium supply, which causes other problems.)

- Also drink plenty of milk and juice. Avoid caffeine. And absolutely no alcohol.

Express yourself:
Right now, fill a big glass with cold water and drink it without setting the glass down.

28.
Eat foods that are good for you.

- Grief is hard work, emotionally, spiritually and physically. Your body will feel better if you give it good fuel, especially now.

- You may be in the habit of eating a lot of fast food or junk food. Instead of telling yourself you need to stop, simply try to eat two servings of fruit and three servings of vegetables every day. Also get in some whole grains if you can. If you eat these foods, you won't be as hungry when you hit McDonald's drive-through next time.

- Ask a parent to prepare your favorite dinner sometime soon. Offer to help cook and clean up.

Express yourself:
Prepare a simple, healthy meal or snack after school today. Be sure to include at least one fruit or vegetable.

29.
Sleep tight.

- Most teenagers sleep a lot. Your body needs so much rest because it's growing and changing like crazy right now.

- Your grief may make you even more tired. Mourning is fatiguing work. It's normal for people in mourning to feel extra exhausted. Sleep renews and refreshes not only our bodies, but our minds and spirits.

- Or you may find that you can't sleep well right now. Maybe your thoughts about the death are keeping you awake. Maybe you're having bad dreams. It's also normal for your sleep to be disturbed for awhile.

- Sleep when you're tired. Go to bed early and sleep in when you can. Take naps.

Express yourself:

Go to bed an hour or two earlier tonight. Curl up in bed with
a book or listen to soothing music. If you're drowsy, let yourself
drift off to sleep. Sleep tight.

30.
If the person died after a lengthy illness, understand that you'll still need to mourn.

- When someone you love is terminally ill—and perhaps in pain or discomfort for days on end—you may well feel relief when the death occurs. This is normal and natural and in no way equals a lack of love for the person.

- In cases of terminal illness, family members and friends typically start mourning the loss well before the actual death. But this doesn't mean you'll be "over it" when the death occurs. You still have a need and right to mourn in the coming weeks, months and years.

- Even when you know someone is dying, you can never really be prepared for the death. We're never really ready for the death of someone we love. The death may still feel unreal and shocking to you.

Express yourself:
Close your eyes and remember what the person was like before the illness took hold. Write about these memories in your journal.

31.

If the person died because of an illness, learn about and raise money to cure it.

- If the person who died had cancer, heart disease, multiple sclerosis or another illness, maybe it would help you to read up on the illness' causes and current research into prevention or cures.

- You could channel your grief into volunteering for an organization that funds medical research, such as the American Cancer Society or the SIDS Alliance.

- Many such organizations conduct annual neighborhood funding drives. Maybe with your parent's help you could be in charge of fundraising for your neighborhood.

Express yourself:

Do some research online today and learn more about the illness and how many people it affects each year.

32.

If the person who died was killed accidentally, talk to someone about your "if-onlys."

- Car accidents, airplane crashes, sporting accidents and other sudden and unexpected events sometimes claim the lives of people we love—often young people whom we feel were too young to die.

- When someone dies suddenly and without warning, you may feel regretful or guilty that you didn't prevent the death somehow (even though you couldn't have).

- "If only I had called, he might have missed that flight." "If only I'd told him the roads were icy . . . " "If only I'd told him I loved him one last time."

- These are normal and natural feelings of regret. Expressing them will help you move on in your grief journey.

Express yourself:
Has an "if-only" been bugging you since the death? Talk to someone about it today.

33.
If the person who died completed suicide, know that he made his own choice.

- No one drives anyone else to complete suicide. A mental health disorder, a loss of hope, feelings of victimization, entrapment or self-loathing are some reasons why people choose to take their own lives.

- It's important for you to know that you or others are not to blame for someone else's decision to commit suicide.

- Still, after a suicide survivors often feel a ton of difficult feelings. Writing or talking about your natural feelings will help. Remember—you are not at fault for this death.

Express yourself:
With your friends or in your journal, talk or write about the thoughts and feelings you have had since the death of someone to suicide. Why did this happen? What feelings do you have toward the person who died?

34.

Release your anger in constructive ways.

- Sometimes you may feel angry over losing someone you love. Anger is part of grieving and is a healthy emotion. What you do with your anger, though, can sometimes be harmful.

- Develop ideas for constructively expressing anger. Learn to recognize the early physical symptoms of approaching anger—tensed muscles, rising body temperature, a clenched jaw, stomach discomfort. When you first notice these signs, go to a place where you can release your anger without harm to yourself or anyone else.

- If you're angry at the person who died, at God or at someone who may have contributed to the death, reach out to a trusted adult with whom you can explore your feelings. Remember—express, don't repress, feelings of anger. Just find outlets that won't harm you or anyone else.

Express yourself:

Dance, run, flail your arms, jump rope, smash a tennis ball against a wall, punch a pillow. Strenuous physical activity can be the best outlet for anger. It also increases your endorphins—naturally occurring chemicals that make you feel better.

35.

If you have a pet, let her comfort you.

- Pets can sense your feelings. They often show they care by wanting to be close to you when you're feeling blue. The presence of a pet and the unconditional love she feels for you can be a tremendous comfort when you're grieving.

- Enjoy the quiet presence of your pet. Know that you're safe telling her how you're feeling. She won't judge you or offer advice. She'll just be there for you.

Express yourself:

Allow yourself to cry in front of your pet. Stroke her. Tell her how much she means to you and how glad you are that she's here.

36.
Know that it's normal to grieve when your pet dies.

- Losing an animal friend can be as painful as losing a person you loved. Your pet's unconditional love for you made him special. When you're a teenager, your pet can be a real ally.

- When you lose that friend, you're allowed to feel sad, empty, and mad at the world. Let yourself mourn your pet the same way you'd mourn the loss of anyone else you loved. Don't feel silly or ashamed of your intense feelings. Everyone feels deep sadness and pain when a beloved pet dies.

Express yourself:

Make a scrapbook about your pet. Include photos and some of your favorite memories and mementos. Write about your pet as a friend, confidante, and source of comfort, joy, support, and humor.

37.
Honor your pet.

- Studies have shown that the bond that forms between people and their companion animals can be as strong, or even stronger, than bonds with humans. Pets are unique in accepting us as we are. One reason we love them is because they don't judge or criticize.

- When you lose a pet, honor her by participating in a memorial service. Ask your parents and siblings to join in. Take turns saying goodbye and describing the ways she touched your lives.

Express yourself:

Talk to your family about getting a memorial plaque in honor of your pet. Place it in your yard, perhaps on a bench or a fencepost. Visit the area where you've memorialized your pet. Reflect on the fun times you enjoyed with her.

38.
Memorialize the person who died.

- You can probably remember the person who died in lots of different ways. Reflecting on her special qualities may make you sad at first, but this is a good way to keep her spirit alive and honor her life. Was she understanding? Funny? Artistic? Smart? Offbeat?

- Choose your favorite characteristics. Then think of a tangible way to express them. Pour yourself into creating something that will be a tribute to the person who's died.

- You could paint a painting, write a poem, build a garden bench, volunteer in her honor—anything that pays tribute to her unique life and personality is fitting.

Express yourself:
Write a poem or a song, create a dance, sculpt clay, paint a picture. Dedicate your creation to the life and memory of the person you've lost.

39.

Contribute to a gift that lasts forever.

- Perpetuity means forever. People sometimes create scholarship funds so that each year a deserving student can receive the gift of education. Others may donate to buildings, research, the arts and other projects that benefit humanity. Sometimes the family of a person who died will establish a memorial fund in her name.

- You can donate to a cause, a scholarship, a project, or a memorial fund in the name of the person who died. A gift in perpetuity is a way of immortalizing the name and memory of the person who died and of ensuring that something positive comes out of her death.

Express yourself:

Find out if a memorial fund has been created for the person who died. Consider donating to it or to another meaningful cause. If a fund has not been started, consider being the person who starts one. If you need help, ask a trusted adult to assist you.

40.
Plant a tree.

- Having something nearby that represents life and beauty is another way to perpetuate the memory of someone you've lost.

- Plants, fruit trees, flowering bushes, and other types of greenery remind us of the beauty of nature and her cycles of life, death, and rebirth. You can honor the memory of the person you've lost to something you plant outdoors. In nurturing that plant, you also nurture yourself and the spirit of someone you loved.

- Invite others who loved the person who died and hold a brief ceremony while you plant the tree. Ask each person to share a memory as they shovel in a few spadesful of dirt.

Express yourself:

At a nursery or garden store, choose a living plant, small tree or bush that appeals to you. Plant it in a special place where you'll see it often. Care for the plant in memory of the person who died.

41.
Take on a mission.

- When one mother got angry about a drunk driver killing her teen-age daughter, she took action and formed Mothers Against Drunk Driving. Now a nationally recognized organization, MADD has thousands of members who work to reduce the number of deaths caused by drunk drivers.

- Thousands of organizations exist to improve our quality of life and to raise awareness about important issues. Getting involved with such an organization is one way you can help to bring about positive change.

- Some examples: March of Dimes, American Cancer Society, American Heart Association, Cystic Fibrosis Foundation, Habitat for Humanity, your state organ donor organization.

Express yourself:
Talk to your counselor, search the Internet, or read newspapers and magazines to find out about different causes. Look into joining one that you feel passionate about.

42.
Volunteer.

- Giving of yourself and your time is the most precious gift you can give—and can also help you to move forward. Often, you will find that in return you receive more than you gave.

- An expression of gratitude, a smile, or a tender touch from someone who appreciates your presence can make you realize your value and the connection you share with other human beings.

- Ask a friend or grown-up to volunteer with you so you won't feel so awkward at first.

Express yourself:
Offer to donate a couple of hours of your time each week to helping at a local homeless shelter, a church or place of worship, a nursing home, or other place needing volunteers. Keep a journal of your experience and what you gain from it.

43.
Do something fun.
Dedicate it to the one you lost.

- If the person who died were still alive, chances are you'd spend some time having fun together. Having fun is one of the most joyful ways to express your alive-ness.

- It may seem difficult to have fun now, but you can—and you deserve to. Gather your friends and agree to do something fun together in honor of the person who died.

- Having fun will allow you to take a "time-out" from your grief and that will help you survive right now.

Express yourself:
Go to an amusement park, dance in the rain, have a water balloon fight, play laser tag or whatever sounds fun to you. Throw yourself, heart and soul, into the activity.

44.
Take the person who died on an outing.

- Even though someone you loved has died, she's never completely gone. You think about her a great deal right after her death. Years later, you will still carry her inside you and be reminded of her by certain sights, sounds, and smells.

- Right now, and for the rest of your life, you have the ability to appreciate and enjoy the spiritual presence of the person who died. Visualize her. Speak her name. Hum a song that reminds you of her. Recognize and acknowledge things that remind you of her.

Express yourself:
Go for a walk, a bike ride or out on a photo shoot, and invite along the person who died. Point out and photograph things that strike you and tell her why you're shooting them. Create an album or scrapbook of that experience.

45.
Know that the one you lost is with you in spirit.

- Losing someone close to you can sometimes lead to feelings of abandonment, desolation, or despair. You may at times feel that life isn't worth living. It can be hard to listen to well-intentioned but misguided people who encourage you to "keep your chin up" or "think about your future."

- Maybe it will help to think about this: The person who died wanted the best for you when he was alive. His spirit is with you now, and he still wants only the best for you. Make him proud. Make him smile. Make his spirit sing.

- Not all relationships are good ones, however. If the person who died was unkind or even abusive to you, it's OK to feel relief and a sense of freedom.

Express yourself:
In your journal, write about the best things that you and the person who died brought out in each other.

46.
Do something you're good at.

- Have people told you you're good at this or that? Next time you're complimented in this way, take it to heart!

- Knowing you're good at something can help you believe in and love yourself, even if you're feeling low right now.

- Skateboard. Make someone laugh. Bake cookies. Draw. Tutor a friend in math or English. Do whatever you're good at.

- Be on the lookout for talents or gifts you may possess but haven't yet discovered in yourself.

Express yourself:
Make a list of five things you're good at. Do one of them today and afterwards, be aware of how it makes you feel.

47.
Do something you're not so good at.

- Doing something you're not so good at helps you learn to think with an open mind and be flexible.

- Just because you're not naturally talented at something doesn't mean you can't learn. Did you know that Michael Jordan was cut from his high school basketball team when he was a sophomore?

- Try not to get frustrated. Just concentrate on learning and having fun.

Express yourself:
I bet you have a friend who likes to do something you're not so good at. Surprise him today by asking him to do it with you and teach you a few pointers.

48.
Do something to improve yourself.

- Losing someone you love is not unlike ending a chapter in the book that is your life. The person who died was, and will continue to be, a meaningful influence in your journey. But now you must go on without his physical presence.

- This may be a good time to choose a new behavior or challenge that will help you grow into the person you want to be. Embarking on a course of self improvement as a tribute to the person you've lost can give you new determination—and a goal that will help you envision and move toward your future.

Express yourself:
Today, resolve to change a bad habit, complete an unfinished project, or learn something new. Write down your goal, a deadline, and the steps you'll take towards your goal this week.

49.
Do something the person who died liked to do.

- What did the person who died like to do? Golf? Garden? Play soccer? Go to the movies? Shop?

- Plan an activity that the person who died would have enjoyed then carry it out in his honor. Think of him while you're doing it. My dad loved tennis, so every time I play tennis or watch it on TV I think of him and feel close to him.

- You could do the activity alone or you could do it with your family or a group of friends.

Express yourself:
Talk to a family member or friend today about planning an activity that the person who died would have enjoyed.

50.
Go surfing.

- The Web can be a great resource for grief information and support—if you know where to look.

- Try www.beliefnet.com, www.dougy.org, www.hospicefoundation. org, www.solacehouse.org and my website, www.centerforloss.com.

- If you type "teen grief" into your favorite search engine, you'll probably find many other helpful sites.

Express yourself:
Look for grief information on the Web today. Print out a few pages and read it before you go to bed.

51.
Go for a long drive.

- If you have your driver's license (and your parents' permission), go for a long drive by yourself. You don't need to go anywhere, just drive.

- Take a scenic route and stop for a rest when you get tired.

- Don't crank up the CD player; instead, play soft background music or no music at all.

- While you drive, take advantage of the solitude to think about the death and remember the person who died.

Express yourself:
Is there a certain place that reminds you of the person who died? Drive there today and spend some time remembering. Bring a friend if you'd like the company.

52.
Watch the sun rise.

- Getting up early to watch the sun splash color across the sky can change your whole outlook. The sun is a powerful symbol of life and renewal.

- Just getting up earlier than you normally do is a way of taking charge of your life again. Nature puts on a spectacular show and suddenly it's bright and a whole new day lies ahead of you.

- Getting up extra early once in a while also allows you to have a special time of quiet and solitude before your busy day begins.

Express yourself:

Make a date with yourself or a friend to get up before the crack of dawn and go to a park, a mountain top, or other beautiful place to watch the sun come up.

53.
Surround yourself with smells.

- Our sense of smell can be the most powerful where memory is concerned. A whiff of coconut oil might bring back vivid memories of the beach where you splashed and played as a toddler. A certain perfume may bring your grandmother to mind.

- Scents you enjoy can soothe you, energize you, make you feel happy or sleepy. Learn to identify the smells that make you feel good. Then find them and keep them close by.

- What smells remind you of the person who died? How can you keep those smells a part of your life? My grandma used to make the best doughnuts in the world. Now, anytime I go by a bakery I have warm thoughts of her.

Express yourself:
Discover one or two fragrances that appeal to you the most, and buy them in some different forms—incense, perfumes, flowers, scented candles, shampoos, sachets, or essential oils, for example. Use some for your skin and others to scent your room.

54.
Don't techno-escape.

- TV, computer games, the Web, video games—they're lots of fun and they can help us lose ourselves for a while.

- It can be tempting to lose yourself in electronic toys every spare minute, however. It's OK to escape reality now and then, but not too often. Video games and the computer shouldn't take the place of real human beings in your life, especially not now, when you need other people the most.

- If you deny your grief now, it'll grow more powerful and you'll have to deal with it later.

Express yourself:
If you're online all the time, at least use your cyber-powers to search for grief information, e-mail notes to supportive adults or post messages to a teen grief bulletin board or chat room. (Never give out your phone number or address or arrange to meet a cyber contact in person, however.)

55.
Rearrange your room.

- A change of scenery can often lift your spirits and reduce or eliminate negative energy in your environment.

- You can create new scenery in your own personal space simply by rearranging your room. Play music as you work. Visualize how you want your room to look and feel. Throw away or give away stuff you no longer want or need. With permission, paint your walls a soothing or energizing color. Megan, my pre-teen daughter, and I just painted her room tranquil blue and talked about how it feels like living in the clouds.

- Look into the principles of feng shui (pronounced fung shway), which is an Eastern philosophy of interior design and how it affects our lives. According to feng shui, how and where your bed is placed, for example, affects your happiness.

Express yourself:
Find new ways to display those things you love most. Discover new and pleasant views. Create a quiet corner where you can read, relax, or listen to music. Feel the lightness of your renewed place.

56.
Light a candle.

- A votive candle is a small, short candle that is lit in devotion or gratitude. You may have seen rows of votive candles in churches. People often light these candles in memory of someone they love. The flame is a symbol of the spirit, the light a sign of hope or illumination.

- First, ask your parents for permission to keep candles in your room. Then find a candle that's nestled inside a glass or other fireproof container. Choose one with a color and scent you enjoy or has meaning for you. Place the candle in your room near a photo of the person who died.

Express yourself:
Light the candle in memory of the one you've lost.
Remember her and honor her with thoughts of gratitude for
the time you shared together.

57.
Buy a new poster.

- Often, we choose artwork because of the way it makes us feel. You may feel soothed by certain colors, brushstrokes or subjects. A mountain view, a seascape, a wildflower meadow, or a sunset may bring you peace. A photo of your favorite musician or group might make their music come alive inside you.

- Artwork often speaks to us in ways that words can't. Look for a poster that captures some aspect of your grief or of the person who died.

Express yourself:
Losing someone you love makes you see the world differently. Choose a new poster for your room that is especially meaningful or comforting to you now.

58.
Get a plant for your room.

- Plants have personality. They respond to nurturing with new growth or blossoms or by simply being beautiful.

- In subtle ways, a plant that you care for takes care of you, too. It purifies the air you breathe. It softens your manmade environment by infusing it with a touch of nature. It becomes a quiet companion.

Express yourself:
Choose a plant that you find beautiful or that reminds you of the person who died. Give it a special place in your room. Learn about your plant and care for it.

59.
Listen to music.

- Music has the ability to move us in indescribable ways. Whether it's vocals or just instruments, music seems to touch our very core. Different kinds of music evoke different emotions and can make us feel soothed, energized, happy, melancholy, joyful, serene.

- You may find that sounds of nature—the ocean, loons, a rainstorm—accompanied by instruments are especially powerful in putting you in touch with your emotions at this time. Certain lyrics or melodies might also express what you feel or put you in a mood you enjoy. Who is your favorite group right now?

Express yourself:
Listen to new CDs, and buy one that feels as though it touches your soul. When you listen to it, try to feel the music. Lose yourself in the way it makes you feel.

60.
Pamper yourself.
If you're a girl, try this.

- It's sometimes easy to neglect yourself when your mind and emotions are preoccupied with something as monumental as the death of someone you loved.

- Take time out to pamper your body. It will feel good and will help soothe your mind and calm your emotions.

- Get a new haircut or a facial. Shop for a special new outfit. Buy a new perfume.

Express yourself:

Give yourself a manicure and paint your nails in a new way. Find some bath salts or oils with a fragrance you enjoy and indulge in a hot bubble bath. Light a candle and play relaxing music while you soak.

61.
Pamper yourself.
If you're a guy, try this.

- Guys don't often think about pampering themselves. When you're dealing with the thoughts and feelings that accompany grief, it's even less likely that you'll think of doing something nice for yourself.

- But taking time out for pampering can make you feel better all the way around. Not only will your body appreciate the kind attention, your mind and emotions will feel calmed as well.

- Get a haircut. Try a new deodorant or cologne. Buy a new shirt.

Express yourself:
Buy some cedar or herbal bath salts and enjoy a long, hot soak surrounded by candles and with relaxing music playing in the background. Afterwards, massage your feet with a moisturizing cream or lotion.

62.
Get a pen pal.

- It helps to have someone to share your thoughts and feelings with. Sometimes it's easier to write about what you're feeling than to talk about it.

- If you don't already have a pen pal relationship, think about starting one. Do you have a friend, a cousin, an older sibling no longer living at home, or someone else with whom you can correspond? Choose someone you trust and feel comfortable opening yourself up to. Agree to confidentiality.

Express yourself:
Send a letter or e-mail to your pen pal. Explain how you're feeling.

63.
Write a letter to the person who died.

- A personal letter is an intimate way to connect with someone. You might have letters from the person who died. Rereading them may make you feel closer to him and bring you comfort.

- Writing a letter to him now can help you continue that feeling of connectedness. Even though the person who died is no longer around physically, the words and sentiments you've shared will always exist.

- Writing a letter to the person who died can also tie up loose ends. If you wanted to say something to him but never had the chance, or if you feel a sense of unfinished business about something, say it now in the form of a letter. Read it aloud at the cemetery or scattering site or share the letter with someone you trust.

Express yourself:
Write a letter to the person who died. Tell him how you feel. Tell him about your day. Write those things you'd want him to know now.

64.
Visit the cemetery.

- Visiting the cemetery isn't creepy, it's an important mourning ritual. It helps us embrace our loss and remember the person who died.

- Memorial Day, Veteran's Day, Mother's Day and Father's Day are traditional days to visit the cemetery and pay respects. You might also want to go on the birthday of the person who died or the anniversary of the death.

- If the body was cremated, you may want to visit the scattering site or columbarium.

- Ask a friend or family member to go with you. You may feel comforted by their presence. Or, if it feels right for you, go alone and sit in sacred silence.

Express yourself:
If you can, drop by the cemetery today. Bring a fresh flower and scatter the petals over the grave.

65.
Visit a place of worship.

- Does your family belong to a church or other place of worship? Do you attend services regularly? You may find comfort and meaning in the words and music you hear there.

- Contemplating your spirituality during worship services also helps you search for the meaning of life and death, which is Mourning Need #5 (See Idea 8).

- If your family doesn't belong to a church, maybe you could attend services with a friend's family and see how you like it.

Express yourself:
Attend a worship service sometime this week.
Pray. Sing. Lift up your grief.

66.
Pray.

- Studies have shown that prayer can help people heal.

- If you believe in a higher power, pray.

- Pray about the person who died. Pray for your questions about life and death to be answered. Pray for help in dealing with the pain you feel. Pray for others affected by this death.

- Many churches or places of worship have youth groups. Now may be a good time to get involved in one if you're not already. Being around spiritual people can be very restorative.

Express yourself:
Bow your head right now and say a silent prayer. Don't worry if you don't really know how to pray or what to say. Just let your thoughts flow naturally.

67.
Own your feelings.

- Grief often involves a wide spectrum of feelings ranging from disbelief and depression to anger, guilt, frustration, loneliness and more. Experiencing these emotions, and sometimes feeling overwhelmed by them, is a natural part of the grief process.

- Rather than deny or feel victimized by your emotions, learn to recognize and confront them. Naming the feeling and acknowledging it is the first step to dealing with it.

- Know that all the feelings you feel are normal and are often felt by other mourners. You're not weird. You're not the only one. You're not going crazy.

Express yourself:
Identify the feeling. Write it down or say it out loud: "I feel sad," or "I'm so angry right now!" Talk or write about how the emotion affects your body—depleted energy, tensed muscles, feelings of pain or emptiness, for example. Inhale deeply. When you exhale, let the feeling be expressed outside of yourself.

68.
Pour yourself into life.

- Before the death, you probably led an active life filled with school-work, friends, hobbies, sports, and other extracurricular activities. After the person died, you may have lost interest and enthusiasm for many of the activities in your life.

- Giving yourself some down-time immediately after the death can be helpful. Later, living each day to the fullest will help you find continued meaning in life and living.

- You may have heard the Latin expression *carpe diem*, which means "seize the day." Death reminds us that life can be short but oh so very sweet. Seize the day. Make the most of earth's every rotation. Love and be loved.

Express yourself:

Make a pact with yourself to pour yourself into life and give everything you do your full attention and your best shot. If your schedule permits, add a new activity that interests you.

69.
Simplify your life.

- If you're feeling overwhelmed and stressed out by your grief, don't pour yourself into life (Idea 68). Sometimes we need to slow down before we can speed up again.

- Your daily schedule may be jam-packed with school, sports, clubs, a job, family activities. Today's teenagers often have a lot on their plates.

- Simplify. Consider all your commitments in the next few months and decide which you could eliminate and which are truly important to you.

Express yourself:
Make a list of all your commitments. Are there some you truly don't enjoy? Though not all activities are optional (school, for example, and household chores), some are. Consider taking a one month break from an activity that's making you feel stressed right now.

70.
Read.

- When you find a philosophical book that speaks to you, you often lose yourself in it. You also gather ideas and perspectives for dealing with the past and your feelings in the present. You may gain insights into how you will proceed with the rest of your life.

- Websites, bookstores, and libraries are great places to look for books about healing in grief. Religious books, poetry and self-help books can provide comfort and enlightenment.

- A couple to consider: *Straight Talk About Death for Teenagers* by Earl Grollman and *The Grieving Teen: A Guide for Teenagers and Their Friends* by Helen Fitzgerald.

Express yourself:

Ask others—parents, friends, teachers, counselors—for the names of books that have helped them deal with a loss. At a bookstore or library, thumb through some of the suggested books. Choose the one that feels right, then read.

71.
See the world anew.

- "The best thing for being sad is to learn something," says Merlin the Magician to King Arthur in T.H. White's *The Once and Future King*.

- As you begin to reconcile your loss, you may find that you receive a gift of new understanding. Instead of focusing on what you've lost, you may begin to see what you've gained and how you've grown as a compassionate human being. You may also have a better sense of how to comfort others when they are in mourning. This is a gift you can give.

- Your life is forever changed by the death of someone loved—but over time and with the support of others, you may come to realize that in some ways it has changed for the better.

Express yourself:
Notice the things you appreciate now more than ever before. Write about them in your journal. Share them with your family and friends. In what ways have you changed?

72.

Enjoy the creative expression of others.

- Often, the way someone else expresses a sentiment perfectly describes the way you feel. Sometimes someone else's words may give you a new insight or offer consolation, humor, or joy. You may feel your mind's been expanded or your perspective altered.

- Read, listen to, and think about the words and meaning in poems, song lyrics, psalms, cards of encouragement and support, and literature. Which ones affect you most? Which can you apply to your life and your thinking?

Express yourself:

In your journal, copy down words and sentiments that you find especially moving or meaningful. Write about the impact these words have on you.

73.
Ask about someone else's loss.

- Others who have suffered a loss may understand your pain and want to help.

- If you ask, they may tell you about the death of someone they loved or other life losses, such as divorce, learning disabilities, illnesses, family problems or chemical abuse.

- When others share their stories with you, and when you listen attentively, an invisible bond forms. You're not so alone anymore. Suddenly you have a bit more hope, a feeling of compassion, a new perspective.

Express yourself:
When someone opens up to you, it's a gift. Treasure it. Learn from it. Write about it in your journal or talk to someone you trust about any feelings it stirs up in you.

74.
Remember the good times.

- Losing someone you love doesn't mean losing the great memories you have of her. Was there a certain look you gave one another that revealed what you were thinking? Is there a day, a moment, a place, a funny incident that reminds you of her and the special relationship you had?

- Good memories from life help soften painful feelings of death. When you keep these memories alive, you keep the person you loved alive inside you, too.

Express yourself:
Use photos, pictures and words from magazines, and your own creative touches, to make a collage that expresses some of the best times the two of you shared.

75.

Make a memory book or memory box.

- There are many things that remind you of the person who died. A memory book or box lets you preserve and revisit some of your favorite memories.

- Start with a blank scrapbook or a sturdy, attractive box. Design a cover. Fill the book or box with photos, cards, ticket stubs, letters, a lock of hair, dried flowers, poetry, song lyrics, quotes, or anything else that reminds you of the person who died. A memory box can be a random collection of items, including photos, souvenirs, video-tapes, and mementos, or a diorama with elements artistically arranged and glued into place.

Express yourself:

Work on your project a little each day. If you want, turn it into a work of art by making the arrangements meaningful and aesthetically pleasing.

76.
Share the memories.

- Others who knew the person who died have fond memories of special moments with that person. Recalling these memories and sharing them aloud is a way to appreciate the person who died as well as those she touched while she was alive.

- Sometimes when you ask others to share a memory of the person who died, you'll learn something new or hear a story you hadn't heard before. These "new memories" can be very special, like an unexpected gift.

- Create a memory book and ask others to each contribute a page.

Express yourself:

At a memorial service or with others who knew the person who died, write down your favorite memory of that person and ask others to do the same. Then share those memories aloud.

77.

Remember others who had a special relationship with the person who died.

- Your grief will naturally make you focus on yourself and your painful feelings. At times you may feel alone in your grief.

- But think about others who were affected by this death: friends, family, teachers, neighbors.

- Is there someone else who may really be struggling with this death? Maybe you could send this person a note or an e-mail telling her you're thinking of her.

- Trying to understand how others feel is called empathy. Being empathetic will not only help you heal your grief, it will make you a better person.

Express yourself:

Today, get in touch with someone else who's been affected by this death. Ask a parent or other caring adult how you could help this person.

78.
Ignore hurtful advice.

- Sometimes well-meaning friends or relatives will hurt you unknowingly with their words.

- You may be told:
  - I know how you feel. (They don't.)
  - Get on with your life. (You're not ready to.)
  - Keep your chin up. (You have every right to be sad.)
  - You're young; you'll get over this. (Nobody ever "gets over" grief.)
  - Time heals all wounds. (Time helps but you're feeling bad today.)
  - He/she wouldn't have wanted you to be sad. (Death and sadness go hand in hand.)

- Don't take this advice to heart. Such clichés are often offered because people don't know what else to say. If their advice makes you angry, say so, but do realize they're trying to help.

Express yourself:
The next time somebody says something foolish or hurtful to you about the death, let them know. Say, "I'm sure you're trying to help but your advice makes me feel _____."
Be honest without being mean.

79.
Don't be scared by "griefbursts."

- Sometimes, out of nowhere, you will feel a wave of sadness you didn't expect. These "griefbursts" can be scary and painful.

- Even long after the death, something as simple as a sound, a smell or a phrase can remind you of the person who died and trigger a griefburst.

- Allow yourself to experience griefbursts without shame or self-judgment, no matter where and when they occur. It's OK if you start to cry at school or suddenly feel sad when you're hanging out with your friends. If you would like to be alone, just say, "I gotta go" and retreat to your bedroom for a while.

Express yourself:
Create an action plan for your next griefburst. For example, you might drop whatever you're doing and go for a run or write in your journal.

80.
Reach out and touch.

- For many people, physical contact with another human being is comforting. It has been recognized since ancient times as having transformative, healing powers.

- Have you hugged anyone lately? Held someone's hand? Put your arm around another human being?

- Often teenagers, particularly boys, don't like hugging or holding hands with someone else (except maybe a girlfriend or boyfriend). Feeling uncomfortable with touch can be a normal part of growing up. If you feel this way, it's OK not to touch. But maybe you can let others simply sit or be near you.

Express yourself:
Is there someone you feel comfortable hugging or holding hands with? Reach out and touch this person today. Notice how it makes you feel.

81.
Identify your needs. Then ask for help.

- Your needs while you grieve may be greater than at any other time in your life. You might need help taking care of yourself. You may need to be prodded out of bed in the morning. You might need a companion more often than usual—a shoulder to lean on, a receptive ear, someone who can take you places.

- Friends and family want to help. It's up to you to tell them how they can help—and how they can't.

- If you can't seem to concentrate on schoolwork right now, for example, ask a parent or teacher for help. If you're afraid to be alone, ask a friend to hang out with you more often.

Express yourself:
Identify what you need help with. Write down the names of three people you can call whenever you need them. Keep their phone numbers with you; the phone line can sometimes be a lifeline!

82.
Turn to your friends for support.

- Friends are especially important during your teenage years. Your friends can be your greatest support when you are grieving.

- You may not feel like being around people when you're sad or depressed over losing someone. But now, more than ever, friends can come to your aid. Even if you have nothing to say, or your friends don't know how to comfort you, their mere presence can be a source of support and comfort.

- Try to talk to your friends about the death and how it makes you feel. Getting up the courage to talk about it can be hard, but your friends will better understand how to help if you do. And expressing your grief helps you reconcile your loss.

Express yourself:
Tell your closest friends that you're not feeling yourself and that you value their presence and friendship. Ask them to check in on you to see how you're doing.

83.
Turn to your faith.

- The word "faith" means to believe in something for which there is no proof. For some people, faith means believing and adhering to a set of religious doctrines. For others, faith is belief in God or a spirit or force that is within us or outside of us.

- Regardless of your religious views, turn now to your faith. Faith offers a way to understand, and bear, the difficulties of both life and death. Faith also can be an assurance that with death come peace and serenity.

- Do you believe in God? What do you believe happens after death? Talk about these issues with a parent or other adult you trust.

Express yourself:
Attend church or go to a place of sanctuary where you can share, or be alone with, your beliefs. Ask to be relieved of your emotional burden. Ask for peace for the person who died and for yourself.

84.
Turn to your family.

- You may not feel like confiding in your family right now. That's normal for teenagers.

- But still, your family loves you and wants what's best for you. During the course of your life, your friends may come and go but your family is forever.

- Allow your family to be there for you. Let them in.

- If you have brothers and sisters, they may feel scared by your grief. They might be worrying about you or upset because they don't understand what you're thinking and feeling. Try talking to them instead of pushing them away. They love you.

Express yourself:
Talk to a family member today about how you're feeling. If you can't or don't want to talk to a parent or sibling, how about an aunt or uncle or grandparent?

85.
Help your family mourn.

- Some families are better at mourning than others. Maybe your parents were never taught how to talk about death or mourn openly. Maybe it makes them uncomfortable.

- You can help your family be better mourners. Initiate discussions about the death. Ask your parents and siblings how they're feeling. Talk about the person who died. Display photos of the person who died.

- Suggest mourning activities your family can do together, such as visiting the cemetery or scattering site or planting a memorial tree.

Express yourself:
If your family isn't so good at mourning or helping you mourn, identify an adult who is and confide in that person.

86.
Seek out your school counselor.

- Going back to school can be really hard after you lose someone special. You may not be able to concentrate. You might feel an overwhelming need to cry. Because you're in pain, you may also feel very alone and wonder if anyone understands your confusing thoughts and feelings.

- Your guidance counselor has special skills and experience to help you through thoughts and feelings that come with grief. Even if you just need a place where you can sit quietly or cry, your counselor will understand and give you your space.

- Teachers and coaches can also help, especially if you already have a special relationship with one of them. Confide in this person. Use him as a sounding board.

Express yourself:
Counselors understand the grief process and that people experience grief in their own ways. Seek out your counselor and let him know if you need to talk or just want some time to be alone with your grief.

87.
Join a support group.

- Grief support groups are a wonderful, safe place for teens with a shared experience to talk about their thoughts and feelings. Many teens find the experience extremely healing.

- Sometimes it's easier to talk to other kids than it is to talk to adults. Teen support groups help you do this.

- Your school may have a support group for grieving teens. Ask your school counselor. If not, your local hospice or funeral home may have one.

- Even if a support group doesn't seem like "you," you might find it helpful to give it a try. You may create new friendships with other teens who can truly understand and support you. Oh—and you will feel good about giving them support, too!

Express yourself:
Ask an adult you trust to look into teen grief support groups for you and arrange for you to attend.

88.
Spend time alone.

- You need to reach out to others when you're grieving. Grief is hard and you can't get through it by yourself.

- Still, you will also need alone time as you work on the six needs of mourning. Sometimes you need silence to really hear your inner voice and solitude to really get acquainted with your grief.

- Spend a few minutes alone with your thoughts and feelings every day. Writing in your journal is a good way to accomplish this.

- Some teenagers have the tendency to spend too much time alone. Don't lock yourself up in your bedroom day after day. Don't become a loner at school.

Express yourself:
Write a poem or a paragraph about who you are. What are your essential qualities? How would others describe you? What are you really like on the inside? What are your hopes and dreams?

89.
Don't numb the pain in unhealthy ways.

- Sometimes the pain of losing someone you love can seem intolerable. For teens, especially, turning to alcohol, drugs, promiscuous sex, or other unhealthy behaviors may seem like a good way to numb the pain.

- Ultimately, these self-abusive behaviors make life more difficult. You'll not only continue to feel bad about losing someone you loved, you'll also regret submitting yourself to unhealthy and disrespectful behaviors. You may also physically hurt yourself or someone else.

Express yourself:
Choose healthy ways to confront your pain. Cry. Spend time with people who love you. Listen to music. Go for a walk. Talk to a counselor. Write. Sleep.

90.

Get help if you're really depressed or thinking about hurting yourself.

- When you're in grief, it's normal to be depressed. It's OK to be deeply sad and to think life really sucks.

- It's not OK to hurt yourself or anyone else, though. If you've been wishing you would die, too, or thinking about how you could end your own life, please tell someone. There are people who will listen to your thoughts and feelings without judging you and who will help you work through them.

- If you're so depressed that you can't get out of bed, can't get any schoolwork done, don't want to be with your friends, and don't want to be with your family, you need some extra help. Tell a parent or a school counselor, or, if you can't bring yourself to talk to them, write them a note.

Express yourself:

If you think you need extra help with your grief, write a note to a parent or a teacher or a school counselor today. Leave the note somewhere they'll find it right away. Better yet, go talk to one of them right this minute.

91.
Look for your grief on certain days.

- Whether you pay close attention to the calendar or not, your cells have a way of reminding you of meaningful dates. You may not understand why you feel sad on a sunny September morning. Then you might realize that this is the anniversary of the day someone you loved died. Or perhaps it's his birthday or a special day you spent together.

- One way to deal with the emotions that often arise with special dates is to plan ahead. Think of ways to commemorate those days. Make special plans in honor of the person who died.

- You might not want to be alone on these days. Invite others to spend time with you.

Express yourself:
Go through your calendar and make a note of all those dates that trigger memories of the person who died. Write down something you can do on those days to celebrate the times you shared.

92.
Know that you are loved.

- There are many, many people who love you—people who want to help you and be there for you.

- Some of them may not know how to help you when you're grieving, but they still love you.

- Think about the people who care about you and how much you matter to them. When you're young, it's sometimes hard to comprehend how very much you mean to other people, but try.

Express yourself:

Try putting yourself in your parents' shoes for a second. You know how you feel about them, but how do they feel about you? Here's what I can tell you as a parent: They love you more than you can comprehend—until the day you have a child. Let them love you and help you.

93.
Know that to love is to one day mourn.

- You are young and yet you have already experienced so much. Your life has already been marked by pain and sadness.

- Yet grief is love's natural partner. If you love you will one day mourn or be mourned.

- Is it worth it? Of course. Life without love is meaningless.

- Love does indeed conquer all. You will come to understand this in the months and years ahead as you learn to reconcile your grief and live and love fully again.

Express yourself:
Consider what your life would have been like had you never known the person who died. Write about this in your journal.

94.
Make plans. Set goals.

- You'll know things are looking bright again when you begin to make plans for your future. Setting goals is the surest way of making plans and dreams come true.

- You have survived the grieving process so far, and you'll continue to integrate the loss and gain strength and understanding from this experience. Use what you've learned to become a better person, to achieve what you'd like to achieve. School counselors, teachers, coaches, and parents are some of the resources you can tap for help in identifying and achieving your goals.

Express yourself:

Check out or buy a book or a tape on setting goals. *The 7 Habits of Highly Effective Teens* by Sean Covey is a good one. Make a list of your short-term and long-term goals. Don't forget to include seemingly impossible dreams. Start visualizing your future.

95.
Understand that healing comes in increments.

- Everyone grieves in different ways and different times. There is no set timetable for grief.

- You may feel that you're healing six months, a year, or two years after losing someone special. Then one day you might feel incredibly sad or lonely because you miss that person so much. Know that this is normal.

- Healing in grief is often a two steps forward, one step back process. You will never completely "get over" the death, but you will, over time and with the support of others, learn to reconcile yourself to it.

- Grief is like waves washing in from the ocean. Sometims they are small and tolerable, yet sometimes when you least expect it a big wave may pull your feet right out from under you.

Express yourself:
Visit the burial site of the person who died. Look again at the photos, journal, scrapbook, or other mementos you created in her memory. Tell her that you miss her.

96.
Count your blessings.

- When you're grieving, it's sometimes easy to forget all the good things about your life.

- I'll bet your life is pretty great in a lot of ways. Can you think of a few of the most important ones?

- I'm not saying you shouldn't be sad right now, because you should. The death of someone loved is the saddest thing in the world.

- But thinking about the people who love you and the things that bring you joy will help you gain perspective.

Express yourself:
In your journal, make a list of the blessings in your life. Put a star next to the ones that most make your life worth living.

97.
Consider the mystical forces of the universe.

- As much as we've learned about our world through science, there's still so much that can't be explained. What's to account for the phone call or letter you suddenly get from someone you haven't seen in awhile but who's been on your mind recently? How do you explain that feeling of already knowing someone you've just met? Or deja vu?

- There's often no explaining why or when things are going to happen. They just happen. Life—and the universe—go on, seemingly with a purpose.

Express yourself:
Make a list of coincidences and unexplained events that have occurred in your life. What were their outcomes? Describe how you felt about those events then and now.

98.
Allow yourself the luxury of time.

- If you are actively mourning this death, you can look forward to the days to come when your grief won't be so hard. As time passes, your painful feelings of loss will be slowly overtaken by warm thoughts and memories of times you spent with the person who died.

- Grief takes time. Don't expect feelings associated with grief—sadness, anger, loneliness, emptiness, guilt, irritability, remorse, and others—to soften right after the person who died is buried or cremated. Grief usually hurts more before it hurts less.

- Record your feelings. Notice how they fluctuate. Give yourself time to heal.

Express yourself:
Keep a grief calendar just for recording your feelings each day. Look back after each week and notice the progress you've made.

99.
Strive to grow through grief.

- Over time, you may find that you are growing emotionally and spiritually because of this death. You may become more compassionate or your faith may become stronger, for example.

- You've probably heard it said that life's greatest gifts grow out of life's most difficult moments. I've found this to be true.

- This isn't to say that we invite or welcome pain just so we can grow. I wish nobody had to grieve, but we do. Our capacity to give and receive love requires that we grieve and mourn.

- But if we do have to grieve and mourn (and we do), let's be aware of the positive changes it brings about in us.

Express yourself:
Ask yourself: In what ways am I a better person
now than I was before the death?

100.
Make a wish.

- Pinnochio's fairy was right: Wishes can make dreams come true if you wish hard enough—and then you work hard enough.

- The person who died can't come back to you, but maybe you have another wish that's really possible.

- What do you wish? Do you wish you could be a better baseball player or gymnast? Do you wish your family would get along better? Among your wishes, which are within your control and which aren't?

- You may have heard The Serenity Prayer: God, grant me the grace to accept the things that cannot be changed, the courage to change the things which should be changed and the wisdom to know the difference.

Express yourself:
Make a list of your most sacred wishes and decide which you have the power to make happen. Pick one and start working to make it a reality today.

A Final Word

Grief is indeed a wise teacher.

Grief teaches us that there is so much to know about ourselves and the world around us.

Grief teaches us that we need to pay attention, to simplify our lives to be open to giving and receiving love.

Grief teaches us that loving and caring for others are our most important tasks here on earth.

Grief teaches us we have only now to let people know that we love them. There is magic and miracles in loving and being loved.

I hope we meet one day and that you will tell me about what grief has taught you. Until then, mourn well.

SEND US YOUR IDEAS FOR HEALING YOUR GRIEVING HEART!

I'd love to hear your practical ideas for helping grieving teens. I may use them in other books someday. Please jot down your idea and mail it to:

Dr. Alan Wolfelt
The Center for Loss and Life Transition
3735 Broken Bow Rd.
Fort Collins, CO 80526
wolfelt@centerforloss.com

I hope to hear from you!

My idea:

_____

_____

_____

_____

_____

_____

_____

_____

My name and mailing/email address:

_____

_____

_____

_____

ALSO BY ALAN WOLFELT

THE HEALING YOUR GRIEVING HEART
JOURNAL FOR TEENS
With a foreword by Brian Griese

Teenagers often don't want to talk to adults—or even to their friends—about their struggles. But given the opportunity, many will choose the more private option of writing. Many grieving teens find that journaling helps them sort through their confusing thoughts and feelings.

Yet few journals created just for teens exist and even fewer address the unique needs of the grieving teen. In the Introduction, this unique journal—written by Dr. Wolfelt and his 14-year-old daughter, Megan—affirms the grieving teen's thoughts and feelings and offers gentle, healing guidance. The six central needs of mourning are explained, as are common grief responses. Throughout, the authors provide simple, open-ended questions for the grieving teen to explore, such as:

• What do you miss most about the person who died?
• Write down one special memory.
• Which feelings have been most difficult for you since the death? Why?
• Is there something you wish you had said to the person who died but never did?
• Describe the personality of the person who died. Tape a photo here, too, if you'd like.

Designed just for grieving teens as a companion to Dr. Wolfelt's best-selling *Healing Your Grieving Heart for Teens: 100 Practical Ideas*, this journal will be a comforting, affirming and healing presence for teens in the weeks, months and years after the death of someone loved.

ISBN 978-1-879651-33-3 • 128 pages • softcover • $11.95
(plus shipping and handling)

ALSO BY ALAN WOLFELT

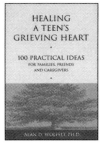

HEALING A TEEN'S GRIEVING HEART: 100 PRACTICAL IDEAS FOR FAMILIES, FRIENDS & CAREGIVERS

If you want to help a grieving teen but aren't sure how, this book is for you. It explains the teen's unique mourning needs, offers real-world advice and suggests realistic activities.

ISBN 978-1-879651-24-1
128 pages • Softcover • $11.95
(plus additional shipping and handling)

Companion
PRESS

All Dr. Wolfelt's publications can be ordered by mail from:
Companion Press
3735 Broken Bow Road • Fort Collins, CO 80526
(970) 226-6050 • Fax 1-800-922-6051
www.centerforloss.com

ALSO BY ALAN WOLFELT

UNDERSTANDING YOUR GRIEF
TEN ESSENTIAL TOUCHSTONES FOR FINDING HOPE AND HEALING YOUR HEART

One of North America's leading grief educators, Dr. Alan Wolfelt has written many books about healing in grief. This new book is his most comprehensive, covering the most important lessons that mourners have taught him in his three decades of working with the bereaved.

In compassionate, everyday language, *Understanding Your Grief* explains the important difference between grief and mourning and explores the mourner's need to gently acknowledge the death and embrace the pain of the loss. This important book also reveals the many factors that make each person's grief unique and the myriad of normal thoughts and feelings the mourner might have. Alan's philosophy of finding "companions" in grief versus "treaters" is explored. Dr. Wolfelt also offers suggestions for good self-care.

Throughout, Dr. Wolfelt affirms the readers' rights to be compassionate with themselves, lean on others for help, and trust in their innate ability to heal.

ISBN 978-1-879651-35-7 • 176 pages • softcover • $14.95

Companion
PRESS

All Dr. Wolfelt's publications can be ordered by mail from:
Companion Press
3735 Broken Bow Road • Fort Collins, CO 80526
(970) 226-6050 • Fax 1-800-922-6051
www.centerforloss.com

ALSO BY ALAN WOLFELT

THE UNDERSTANDING YOUR GRIEF JOURNAL

EXPLORING THE TEN ESSENTIAL TOUCHSTONES

Writing can be a very effective form of mourning, or expressing your grief outside yourself. And it is through mourning that you heal in grief.

The Understanding Your Grief Journal is a companion workbook to *Understanding Your Grief.* Designed to help mourners explore the many facets of their unique grief through journaling, this compassionate book interfaces with the ten essential touchstones. Throughout, journalers are asked specific questions about their own unique grief journeys as they relate to the touchstones and are provided with writing space for the many questions asked.

Purchased as a set together with *Understanding Your Grief,* this journal is a wonderful mourning tool and safe place for those in grief. It also makes an ideal grief support group workbook.

ISBN 978-1-879651-39-5 • 112 pages • softcover • $14.95
(plus additional shipping and handling)

Companion
PRESS

All Dr. Wolfelt's publications can be ordered by mail from:
Companion Press
3735 Broken Bow Road • Fort Collins, CO 80526
(970) 226-6050 • Fax 1-800-922-6051
www.centerforloss.com

ALSO BY ALAN WOLFELT

THE JOURNEY THROUGH GRIEF: REFLECTIONS ON HEALING
Second Edition

This revised, second edition of *The Journey Through Grief* takes Dr. Wolfelt's popular book of reflections and adds space for guided journaling, asking readers thoughtful questions about their unique mourning needs and providing room to write responses.

The Journey Through Grief is organized around the six needs that all mourners must yield to—indeed embrace—if they are to go on to find continued meaning in life and living. Following a short explanation of each mourning need is a series of brief, spiritual passages that, when read slowly and reflectively, help mourners work through their unique thoughts and feelings.

"The reflections in this book encourage you to think, yes, but to think with your heart and soul," writes Dr. Wolfelt. "They invite you to go to that spiritual place inside you and, transcending our mourning-avoiding society and even your own personal inhibitions about grief, enter deeply into the journey."

Now in softcover, this lovely book is more helpful (and affordable) than ever!

ISBN 978-1-879651-11-1 • 176 pages • softcover • $16.95
(plus additional shipping and handling)

Companion
P R E S S

All Dr. Wolfelt's publications can be ordered by mail from:
Companion Press
3735 Broken Bow Road • Fort Collins, CO 80526
(970) 226-6050 • Fax 1-800-922-6051
www.centerforloss.com

ALSO BY ALAN WOLFELT

WHEN YOUR PET DIES
A GUIDE TO MOURNING, REMEMBERING AND HEALING

When your pet dies, you may struggle with your grief. You may feel overwhelmed at the depth of your sadness. This book affirms the pet owner's grief and helps you understand why your feelings are so strong. It also offers practical suggestions for mourning—expressing your grief outside of yourself—so that you can heal. Ideas for remembering and memorializing your pet are also included.

Dr. Wolfelt has been a dog lover and owner for a long time, suffering the loss of his Husky several years ago. Many have been asking Dr. Wolfelt to write a book about pet loss to add to his comprehensive list of publications about grief. Here it is—in his compassionate, practical, inimitable style.

ISBN 978-1-879651-36-4 • 96 pages • softcover • $9.95
(plus shipping and handling)

Companion
PRESS

All Dr. Wolfelt's publications can be ordered by mail from:
Companion Press
3735 Broken Bow Road • Fort Collins, CO 80526
(970) 226-6050 • Fax 1-800-922-6051
www.centerforloss.com